MACHINES CLOSE-UP

MODERN MILITARY
AIRCRAFT

Daniel Gilpin and Alex Pang

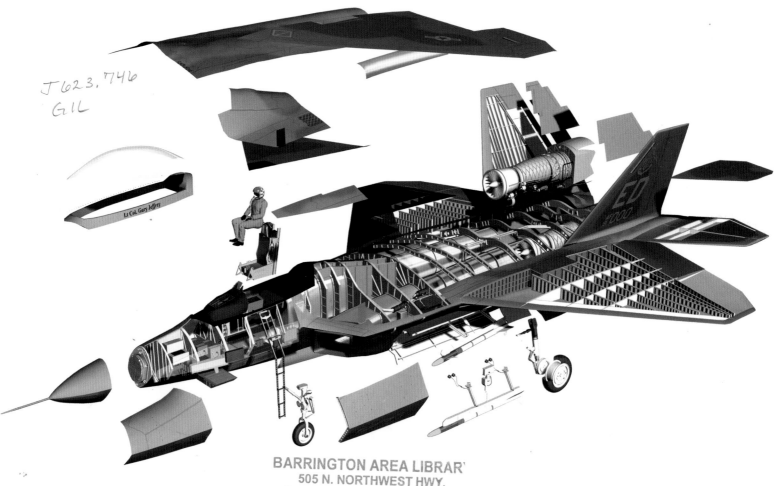

Lt. Col. Gary Jeffrey

ED
#0000

Marshall Cavendish
Benchmark

New York

Website: www.marshallcavendish.us

This publication represents the opinions and views of the author based on
Daniel Gilpin's and Alex Pang's personal experience, knowledge, and
research. The information in this book serves as a general guide only. The
author and publisher have used their best efforts in preparing this book and
disclaim liability rising directly and indirectly from the use and application of
this book.

Other Marshall Cavendish Offices:
Marshall Cavendish International (Asia) Private Limited, 1 New Industrial
Road, Singapore 536196 • Marshall Cavendish International (Thailand) Co
Ltd. 253 Asoke, 12th Flr, Sukhumvit 21 Road, Klongtoey Nua, Wattana,
Bangkok 10110, Thailand • Marshall Cavendish (Malaysia) Sdn Bhd, Times
Subang, Lot 46, Subang Hi-Tech Industrial Park, Batu Tiga, 40000 Shah
Alam, Selangor Darul Ehsan, Malaysia

Marshall Cavendish is a trademark of Times Publishing Limited

First published in 2009 by Wayland
Hachette Children's Books
338 Euston Road
London NW1 3BH
Wayland Australia
Level 17/207 Kent Street
Sydney, NSW 2000

Copyright © 2009 David West Children's Books

Library of Congress Cataloging-in-Publication Data

Gilpin, Daniel.
Modern military aircraft / Daniel Gilpin and Alex Pang.
p. cm. -- (Machines close-up)
Includes index.
Summary: "Reveals and discusses the intricate internal workings of
modern military aircrafts"--Provided by publisher.
ISBN 978-1-60870-108-7
1. Airplanes, Military--Juvenile literature. I. Pang, Alex. II. Title.
UG1240.G54 2011
623.74'6--dc22
2009043246

Produced by
David West Children's Books
7 Princeton Court
55 Felsham Road
London SW15 1AZ

Editor: Katharine Pethick
Designer: Gary Jeffrey
Illustrator: Alex Pang
Consultant: Steve Parker

The photographs in this book are used by permission and through
the courtesy of :
Abbreviations: t-top, m-middle, b-bottom, r-right,
l-left, c-center.
6r, Isabelle + Stéphane Gallay; 6l, access.denied;
6bl, 7r, U.S. Air force; 8t, Robert Lawton; 8,
Paul Maritz; 9t, hoyasmeg; 9bl, U.S. Air force
photo; 9br, Smudge 9000

Printed in China
135642

CONTENTS

16 F/A-22 RAPTOR

18 B-2 SPIRIT STEALTH BOMBER

20 A-10 THUNDERBOLT

22 EA-6B PROWLER

24 MI-24 HIND MILITARY HELICOPTER

26 AC-130 SPOOKY GUNSHIP

28 V-22 OSPREY

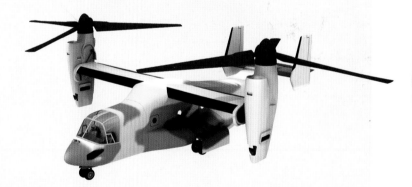

30 FUTURE MACHINES

31 GLOSSARY

32 INDEX

Glossary Words: when a word is printed in **bold**, you can look up its meaning in the Glossary on page 31.

INTRODUCTION

Modern military aircraft include some of the fastest, most technologically advanced, and most expensive vehicles in the world. Each one is designed and its prototype tested over a period of several years before it is produced and used in military service.

GENERATIONS FLY PAST
An F-15 Eagle, F/A-22 Raptor, and an A-10 Thunderbolt fly in formation with a U.S. Mustang fighter plane from World War II.

F/A-22 Raptor

U.S. Mustang

A-10 Thunderbolt

F-15 Eagle

HOW TO USE THIS BOOK

MAIN TEXT

Explains the history of the aircraft and outlines its primary role. Other information, such as which military forces use the aircraft, is also covered here.

SPECIFICATIONS

Gives information about the aircraft's dimensions, speed, and weapon-carrying capacity.

INTERESTING FEATURES

Contains a detailed illustration of the engine or a design feature that makes the aircraft unique. Informative text explains the feature's function.

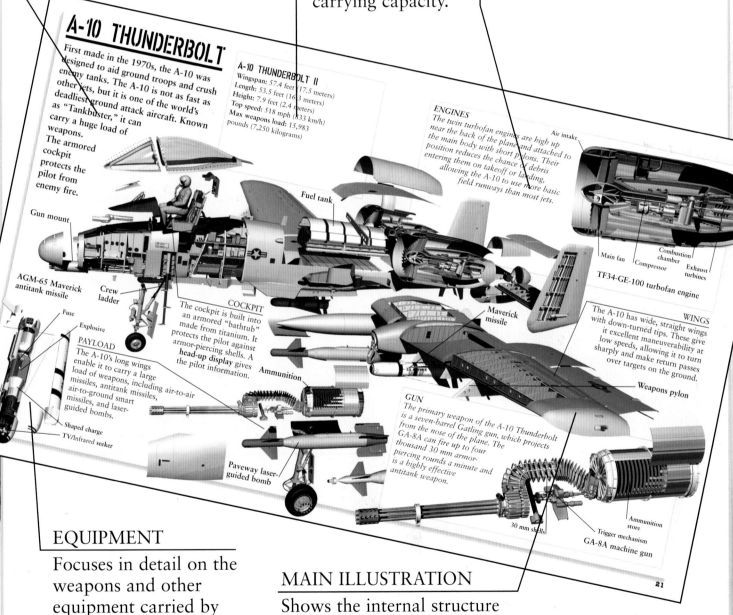

A-10 THUNDERBOLT

First made in the 1970s, the A-10 was designed to aid ground troops and crush enemy tanks. The A-10 is not as fast as other jets, but it is one of the world's deadliest ground attack aircraft. Known as "Tankbuster," it can carry a huge load of weapons. The armored cockpit protects the pilot from enemy fire.

A-10 THUNDERBOLT II
Wingspan: 57.4 feet (17.5 meters)
Length: 53.5 feet (16.3 meters)
Height: 7.9 feet (2.4 meters)
Top speed: 518 mph (833 km/h)
Max weapons load: 15,983 pounds (7,250 kilograms)

ENGINES
The twin turbofan engines are high up near the back of the plane and attached to the main body with short pylons. Their position reduces the chance of debris entering them on takeoff or landing, allowing the A-10 to use more basic field runways than most jets.

Air intake

Main fan   Compressor   Combustion chamber   Exhaust turbines

TF34-GE-100 turbofan engine

Fuel tank

Gun mount

AGM-65 Maverick antitank missile

Crew ladder

COCKPIT
The cockpit is built into an armored "bathtub" made from titanium. It protects the pilot against armor-piercing shells. A **head-up display** gives the pilot information.

Fuse

Explosive

PAYLOAD
The A-10's long wings enable it to carry a large load of weapons, including air-to-air missiles, antitank missiles, air-to-ground smart missiles, and laser-guided bombs.

Shaped charge

TV/Infrared seeker

Ammunition

Maverick missile

WINGS
The A-10 has wide, straight wings with down-turned tips. These give it excellent maneuverability at low speeds, allowing it to turn sharply and make return passes over targets on the ground.

Weapons pylon

GUN
The primary weapon of the A-10 Thunderbolt is a seven-barrel Gatling gun, which projects from the nose of the plane. The GA-8A can fire up to four thousand 30 mm armor-piercing rounds a minute and is a highly effective antitank weapon.

Paveway laser-guided bomb

30 mm shells

Trigger mechanism

GA-8A machine gun

Ammunition store

20

21

EQUIPMENT

Focuses in detail on the weapons and other equipment carried by the aircraft to perform different duties.

MAIN ILLUSTRATION

Shows the internal structure of the aircraft and gives information on the positions of its various working parts.

PROPELLERS TO JETS

The earliest military aircraft were balloons, used for warfare in 1849. During World War I planes replaced balloons, primarily because they were much easier to steer and control.

FLYING CRATES

In World War I, planes, such as the Fokker DR1 were used for **reconnaissance**. In 1914, when battles were fought from trenches, planes could fly over and then give commanders the information they needed to target enemy positions and plan their attacks.

FOKKER EINDECKER
This 1915 fighter was the first with synchronizer gear, which controls gunfire that shoots past the spinning propeller.

SPAD S.XIII
*This French-built **biplane** was a very capable fighter in World War I and so 8,472 were made.*

FOKKER DR1

BOEING P-26
Nicknamed "the peashooter," this was the first all-metal fighter.

STREAMLINED

Early planes were built with little thought given to overall speed. Between the world wars, that began to change. Streamlining became an important feature of plane design. Together with improvements in engine technology, this made planes much quicker.

HANDLEY PAGE 0/100
This World War I bomber was one of the largest early biplanes.

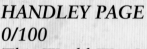

WAR IN THE SKIES

During World War II, aerial combat became increasingly important. The Battle of Britain, an air campaign waged by the German Air Force against the United Kingdom in 1940, proved that aerial superiority decided the fate of nations. In 1939, biplanes were still being used but by 1945, the German Air Force (also known as Luftwaffe) deployed jet fighters in battle.

SPITFIRE
Famous for its role in the Battle of Britain, the Spitfire was capable of doing 606 mph (975 km/h).

SIKORSKY R-4
The world's first mass-produced military helicopter, the R-4, first saw action in 1944.

MESSERSCHMITT BF 109

HEAVY METAL

In the 1920s, military aircraft had metal frames. The development of metal skins, which covered the planes, soon followed, but wood and fabric were still used until after World War II. The extra strength that metal offered was outweighed by its weight and cost.

B-17 FLYING FORTRESS
This massive plane dropped more bombs than any other U.S. aircraft in World War II.

P-47 THUNDERBOLT

THE JET AGE

The first operational jet fighter, the German Messerschmitt ME 262, appeared too late in World War II to make a big impact but it led to a new era in military aircraft design.

MIG 17
This Soviet jet was one of the first with "swept" wings, which reduced drag in order to increase speed.

WING SWEPT

The ME 262 had relatively straight wings, like propeller-driven planes. As jet fighter planes developed, their wings became more swept back. As wing shape changed, so did the position of the engines, which moved into the **fuselage**. Larger planes, such as bombers, kept their engines on the wings.

F-86 SABRE
This U.S. fighter was introduced in 1949. The last active units were retired by the Bolivian Air Force in 1994.

MESSERSCHMITT ME 262

LIGHTNING F.3
*This 1959 British jet fighter was the first plane capable of cruising faster than the speed of sound without **afterburners**.*

PUSHING THE ENVELOPE

The incredible power of the jet engine encouraged experiments with design. Developed for speed in 1947, the YB-49 Flying Wing bomber was ahead of its time. However, due to severe design limitations, especially when bombing, it remained a prototype.

YB-49 FLYING WING

WHIRLYBIRDS

As jets started to replace propellers in planes, another type of aircraft began to appear on military airfields—helicopters. Like jet fighters, the first military helicopters went into action near the end of World War II. Since then they have had a vital role in most air forces.

BELL XV-3
*The first successful **tilt rotor** aircraft, it inspired today's V-22 Osprey.*

HUEY COBRA
First flown in 1965, the Huey remains in active service with several air forces around the world.

F-117 STEALTH FIGHTER

SUKHOI SU-30

TOP GUNS

Today's modern jets are the result of more than a century of military aviation history. Some jets can travel at **supersonic** speeds of more than twice the speed of sound. Others are invisible to **RADAR**.

F/A-22 RAPTOR
The F/A-22 Raptor is state of the art, combining high speed with stealth technology.

EUROFIGHTER TYPHOON
Introduced in 2003, this plane is used by the British Royal Air Force, as well as the Luftwaffe, Italian, and Spanish air forces.

AH-64 LONGBOW APACHE

The AH-64 is the world's most advanced armed helicopter in active service. Designed in 1981, it destroys targets such as tanks. The cockpit and fuel tanks are heavily armored, withstanding hits from rounds of up to 23 mm.

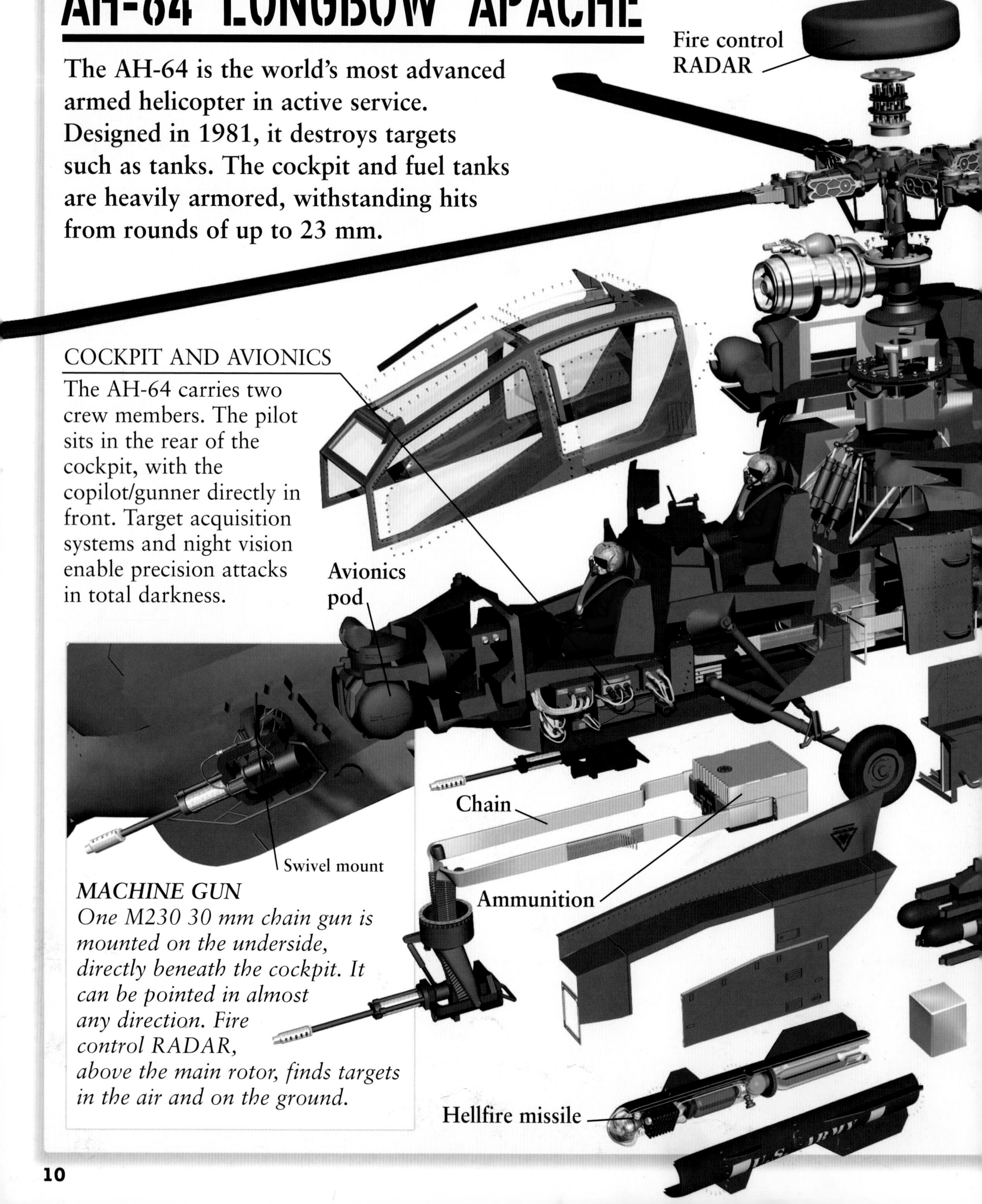

Fire control RADAR

COCKPIT AND AVIONICS

The AH-64 carries two crew members. The pilot sits in the rear of the cockpit, with the copilot/gunner directly in front. Target acquisition systems and night vision enable precision attacks in total darkness.

Avionics pod

Swivel mount

MACHINE GUN

One M230 30 mm chain gun is mounted on the underside, directly beneath the cockpit. It can be pointed in almost any direction. Fire control RADAR, above the main rotor, finds targets in the air and on the ground.

Chain

Ammunition

Hellfire missile

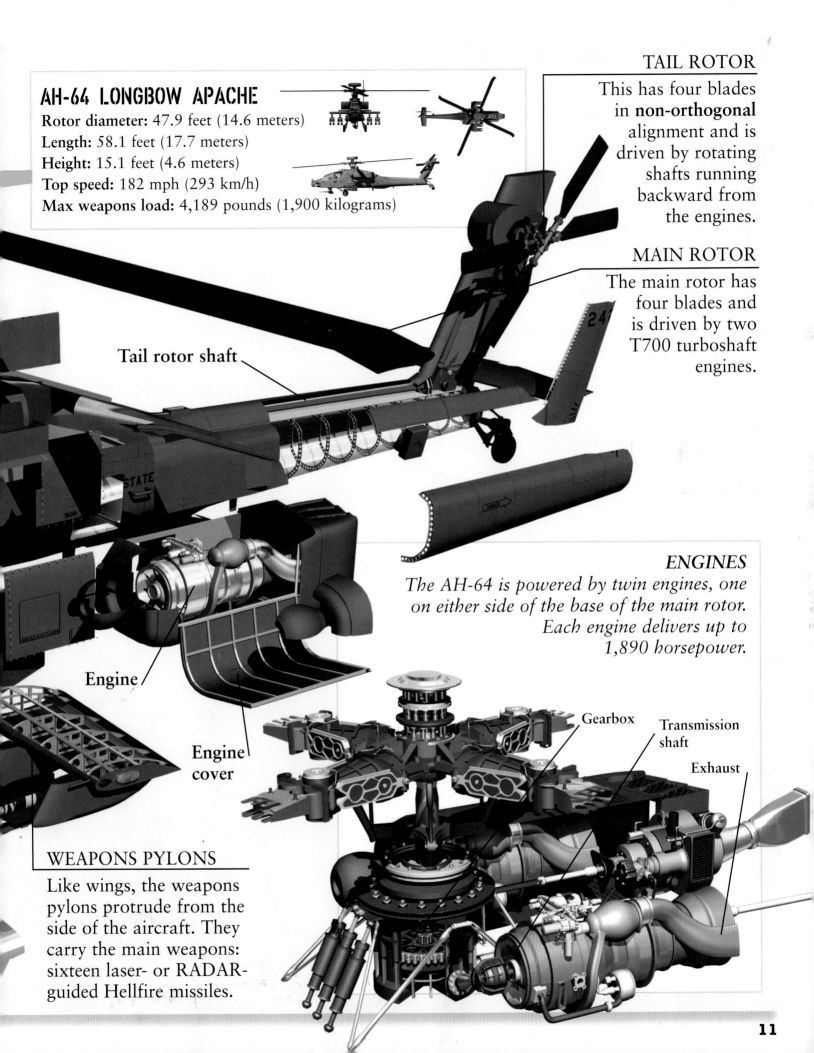

AH-64 LONGBOW APACHE

Rotor diameter: 47.9 feet (14.6 meters)
Length: 58.1 feet (17.7 meters)
Height: 15.1 feet (4.6 meters)
Top speed: 182 mph (293 km/h)
Max weapons load: 4,189 pounds (1,900 kilograms)

TAIL ROTOR

This has four blades in **non-orthogonal** alignment and is driven by rotating shafts running backward from the engines.

MAIN ROTOR

The main rotor has four blades and is driven by two T700 turboshaft engines.

Tail rotor shaft

ENGINES

The AH-64 is powered by twin engines, one on either side of the base of the main rotor. Each engine delivers up to 1,890 horsepower.

Engine

Engine cover

Gearbox

Transmission shaft

Exhaust

WEAPONS PYLONS

Like wings, the weapons pylons protrude from the side of the aircraft. They carry the main weapons: sixteen laser- or RADAR-guided Hellfire missiles.

F-35 LIGHTNING II

Formerly known as the Joint Strike Fighter (JSF), the F-35 Lightning II was commissioned by the U.S. Army to replace the F-16, A-10, F/A-18, and AV-8B fleet of tactical fighter aircraft. The first test versions of the F-35 flew in 2006, and after about five years of development, it went into active service.

F-35 LIGHTNING II

Wingspan: 35.1 feet (10.7 meters)
Length: 50.5 feet (15.4 meters)
Height: 17.4 feet (5.3 meters)
Top speed: 1,200 mph (1,931 km/h)
Max weapons load: 18,012 lbs (8,170 kilograms)

GLIDE BOMB

The F-35 Lightning II can carry a range of weapons. One of these is the AGM-154 glide bomb. It has a range of 81 miles (130 kilometers), so it can be launched at a safe distance from the enemy. It uses GPS to guide it towards its target.

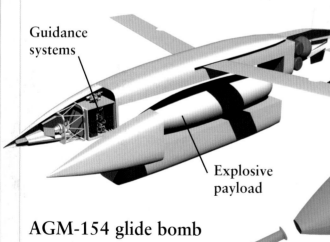

Guidance systems

Explosive payload

AGM-154 glide bomb

Nose spike

COCKPIT

The pilot flies using a right-hand side-stick and a left-hand throttle, and sits on an **ejection seat**.

Helmet screen display system

Cockpit display

Lift fan

SENSORS

The plane's RADAR system is mounted inside its nose. Underneath the nose cone is an **electro-optical targeting** system.

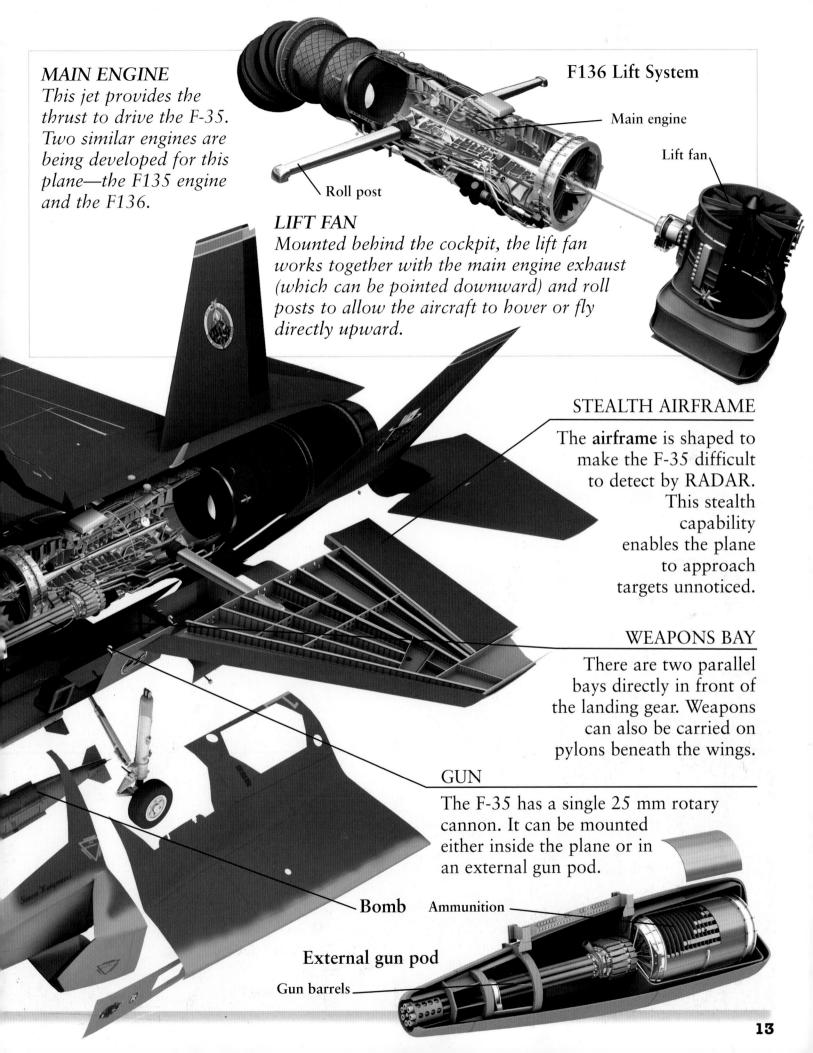

MAIN ENGINE
This jet provides the thrust to drive the F-35. Two similar engines are being developed for this plane—the F135 engine and the F136.

F136 Lift System

Main engine

Roll post

Lift fan

LIFT FAN
Mounted behind the cockpit, the lift fan works together with the main engine exhaust (which can be pointed downward) and roll posts to allow the aircraft to hover or fly directly upward.

STEALTH AIRFRAME

The **airframe** is shaped to make the F-35 difficult to detect by RADAR. This stealth capability enables the plane to approach targets unnoticed.

WEAPONS BAY

There are two parallel bays directly in front of the landing gear. Weapons can also be carried on pylons beneath the wings.

GUN

The F-35 has a single 25 mm rotary cannon. It can be mounted either inside the plane or in an external gun pod.

Bomb   Ammunition

External gun pod

Gun barrels

E-3 SENTRY AWACS

The Boeing E-3 Sentry was produced from 1976 until 1992 and is still in use today. In all, sixty-eight were built for the U.S., U.K., French, Saudi Arabian, and NATO air defense forces. The E-3 Sentry is a flying surveillance center, used mainly for the detection of low-flying aircraft. The letters AWACS stand for Airborne Warning and Control System.

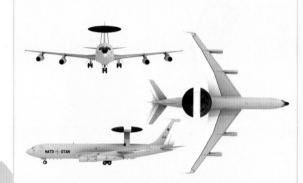

E-3 SENTRY AWACS
Wingspan: 145.7 feet (44.4 meters)
Length: 152.9 feet (46.6 meters)
Height: 41.3 feet (12.6 meters)
Top speed: 531 mph (855 k/h)

FLIGHT DECK
The flight crew includes a pilot and copilot, who fly the aircraft from the deck. The E-3 is a modified Boeing 707 and has similar controls.

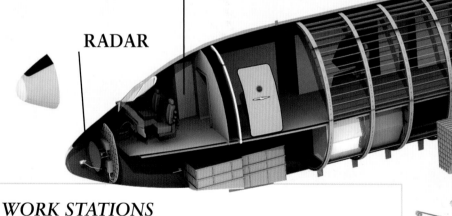

RADAR

Electronics bays

Undercarriage

WORK STATIONS
The E-3 Sentry carries between thirteen and nineteen mission crew, each with their own work station. They carry out surveillance by analyzing data from the RADAR antenna system, which detects both air and sea targets.

Crew at console

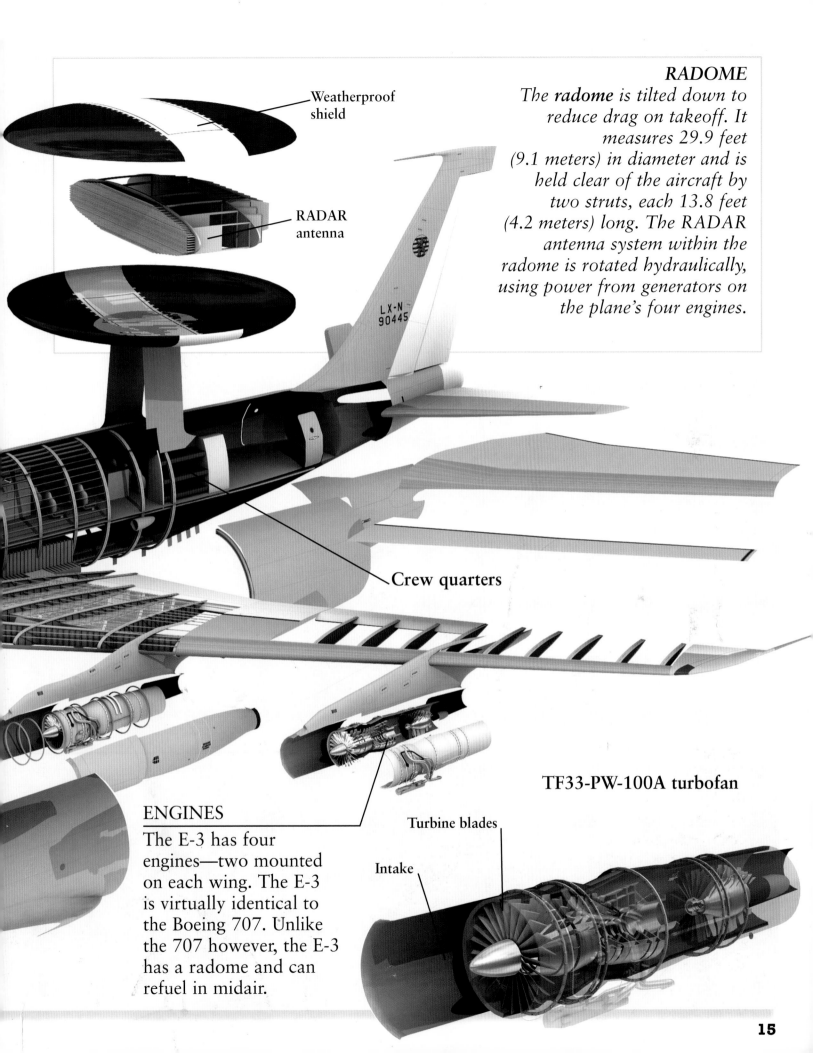

Weatherproof
shield

RADAR
antenna

The **radome** is tilted down to
reduce drag on takeoff. It
measures 29.9 feet
(9.1 meters) in diameter and is
held clear of the aircraft by
two struts, each 13.8 feet
(4.2 meters) long. The RADAR
antenna system within the
radome is rotated hydraulically,
using power from generators on
the plane's four engines.

LX-N
90445

Crew quarters

TF33-PW-100A turbofan

ENGINES

The E-3 has four
engines—two mounted
on each wing. The E-3
is virtually identical to
the Boeing 707. Unlike
the 707 however, the E-3
has a radome and can
refuel in midair.

Turbine blades

Intake

15

F/A-22 RAPTOR

This state-of-the-art fighter was commissioned in 2003 for exclusive use by the U.S. Air Force. The F/A-22 Raptor is a capable but expensive aircraft—each one costs more than $175 million.

F/A-22 RAPTOR

Wingspan: 44.6 feet (13.6 meters)
Length: 62 feet (18.9 meters)
Height: 16.7 feet (5.1 meters)
Top speed: 1,498 mph (2,410 km/h)
Max weapons load: 14,991 pounds (6,800 kilograms)

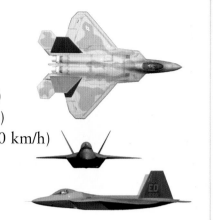

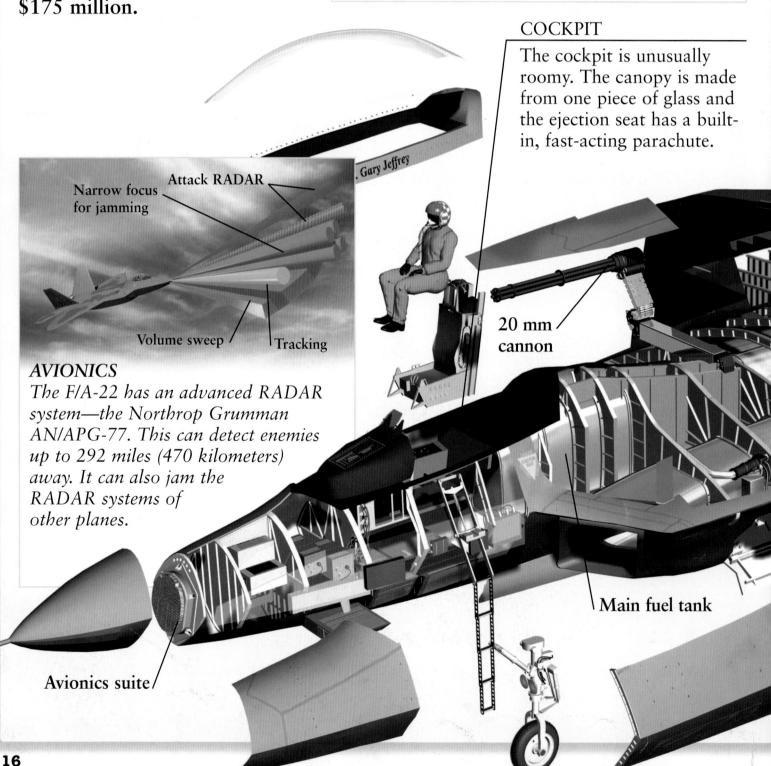

COCKPIT
The cockpit is unusually roomy. The canopy is made from one piece of glass and the ejection seat has a built-in, fast-acting parachute.

. Gary Jeffrey

Narrow focus for jamming

Attack RADAR

Volume sweep

Tracking

20 mm cannon

AVIONICS
The F/A-22 has an advanced RADAR system—the Northrop Grumman AN/APG-77. This can detect enemies up to 292 miles (470 kilometers) away. It can also jam the RADAR systems of other planes.

Main fuel tank

Avionics suite

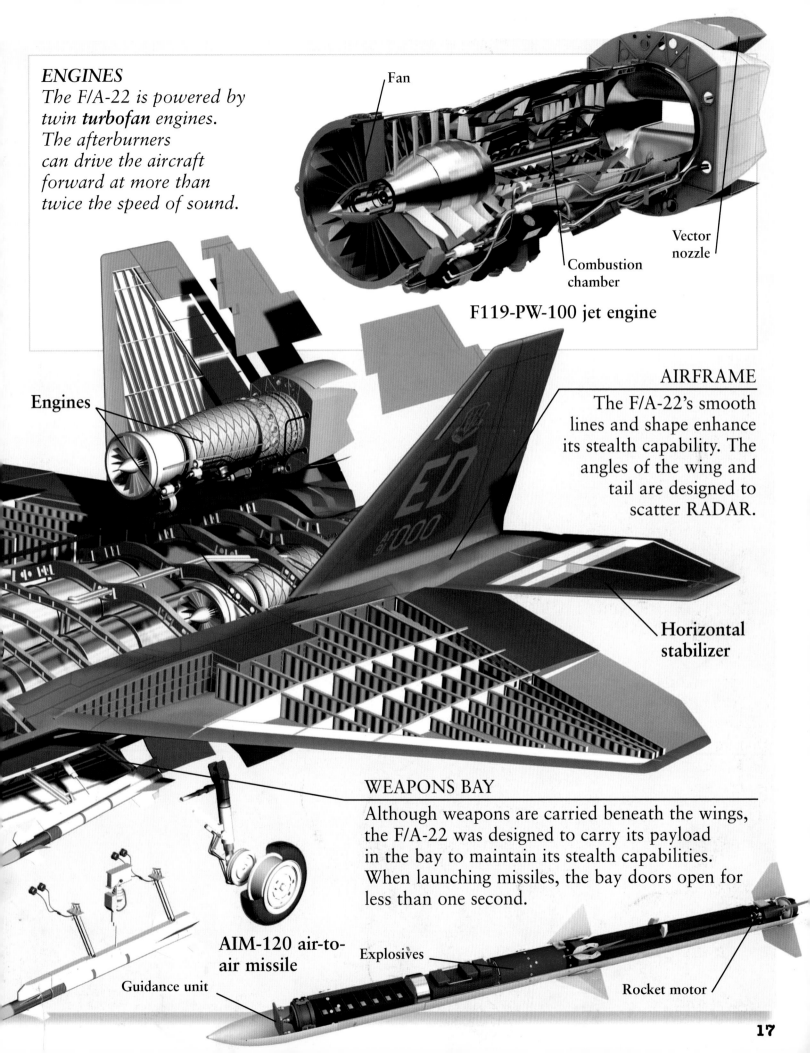

ENGINES
The F/A-22 is powered by twin **turbofan** engines. The afterburners can drive the aircraft forward at more than twice the speed of sound.

Fan

Vector nozzle

Combustion chamber

F119-PW-100 jet engine

Engines

AIRFRAME
The F/A-22's smooth lines and shape enhance its stealth capability. The angles of the wing and tail are designed to scatter RADAR.

Horizontal stabilizer

WEAPONS BAY
Although weapons are carried beneath the wings, the F/A-22 was designed to carry its payload in the bay to maintain its stealth capabilities. When launching missiles, the bay doors open for less than one second.

AIM-120 air-to-air missile

Explosives

Guidance unit

Rocket motor

B-2 SPIRIT STEALTH BOMBER

The cold war prompted the U.S. Air Force to commission the design of the B-2 Spirit Stealth Bomber, but the Soviet Union fell apart before it was completed. A total of twenty-one B-2s were built and have seen action in Kosovo, Afghanistan, and Iraq. The B-2 heavy bomber was designed to carry conventional and nuclear bombs.

STEALTH

The B-2's smooth surface makes it difficult to detect with RADAR equipment. Its stealth paint absorbs RADAR.

FLIGHT DECK

The B-2 has a crew of two. The pilot sits in the left seat and the mission commander in the right. The B-2 is highly automated, allowing one crew member at a time to sleep during long missions.

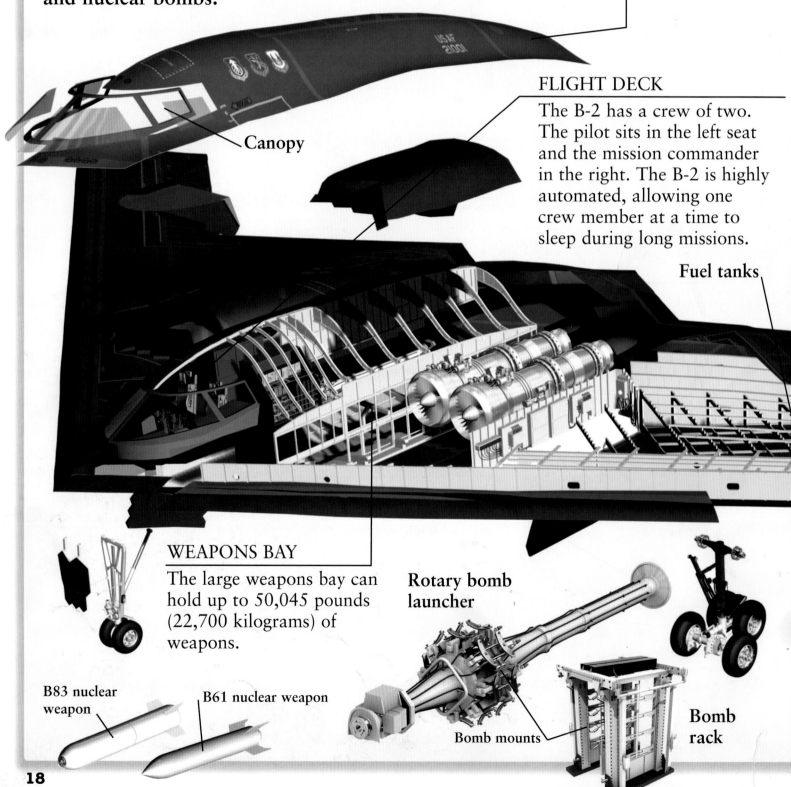

Canopy

Fuel tanks

WEAPONS BAY

The large weapons bay can hold up to 50,045 pounds (22,700 kilograms) of weapons.

Rotary bomb launcher

B83 nuclear weapon

B61 nuclear weapon

Bomb mounts

Bomb rack

F118-GE-100 turbofan engine

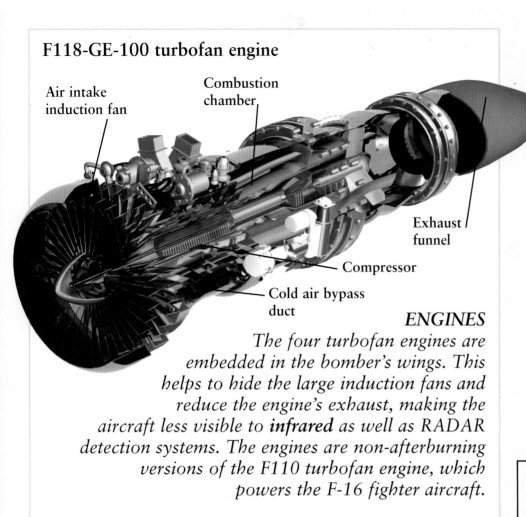

Air intake induction fan

Combustion chamber

Exhaust funnel

Compressor

Cold air bypass duct

NORTHROP GRUMMAN B-2 SPIRIT

Wingspan: 171.9 feet (52.4 meters)

Length: 69 feet (21 meters)

Height: 17.1 feet (5.2 meters)

Top speed: 604 mph (972 km/h)

Max weapons load: 50,045 pounds (22,700 kilograms)

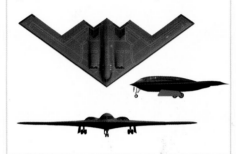

ENGINES

The four turbofan engines are embedded in the bomber's wings. This helps to hide the large induction fans and reduce the engine's exhaust, making the aircraft less visible to **infrared** *as well as RADAR detection systems. The engines are non-afterburning versions of the F110 turbofan engine, which powers the F-16 fighter aircraft.*

AIRFRAME

The B-2's "flying wing" design reduces the number of leading edges to improve its stealth. The materials in the fuselage are top secret. Computer-controlled flying systems make it more stable.

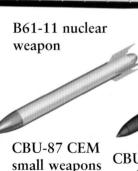

B61-11 nuclear weapon

GQM-113 missile

Joint Stand-Off Weapon (JSOW)

CBU-87 CEM small weapons dispenser

CBU-89 Gator small weapons dispenser

GBU-31 2,000 pound Joint Direct Attack Munition (JDAM)

Mk 84 2,000-pound bomb

PAYLOAD

The B-2 is designed to carry a wide variety of bombs, including up to sixteen B61 or B83 nuclear weapons. During the 1999 conflict in Kosovo it became the first aircraft to carry and deploy GPS satellite guided JDAM "Smart Bombs."

A-10 THUNDERBOLT

First made in the 1970s, the A-10 was designed to aid ground troops and crush enemy tanks. The A-10 is not as fast as other jets, but it is one of the world's deadliest ground attack aircraft. Known as "Tankbuster," it can carry a huge load of weapons. The armored cockpit protects the pilot from enemy fire.

A-10 THUNDERBOLT II
Wingspan: 57.4 feet (17.5 meters)
Length: 53.5 feet (16.3 meters)
Height: 7.9 feet (2.4 meters)
Top speed: 518 mph (833 km/h)
Max weapons load: 15,983 pounds (7,250 kilograms)

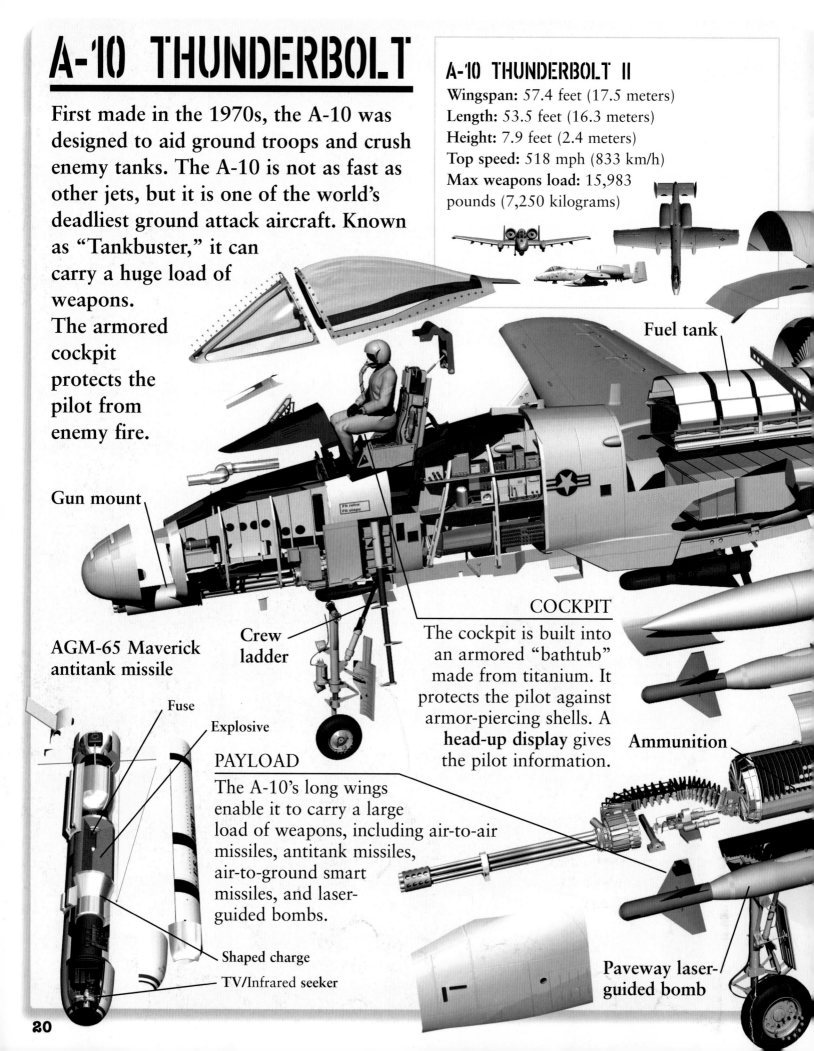

Fuel tank

Gun mount

AGM-65 Maverick antitank missile

Crew ladder

Fuse

Explosive

PAYLOAD
The A-10's long wings enable it to carry a large load of weapons, including air-to-air missiles, antitank missiles, air-to-ground smart missiles, and laser-guided bombs.

Shaped charge

TV/Infrared seeker

COCKPIT
The cockpit is built into an armored "bathtub" made from titanium. It protects the pilot against armor-piercing shells. A **head-up display** gives the pilot information.

Ammunition

Paveway laser-guided bomb

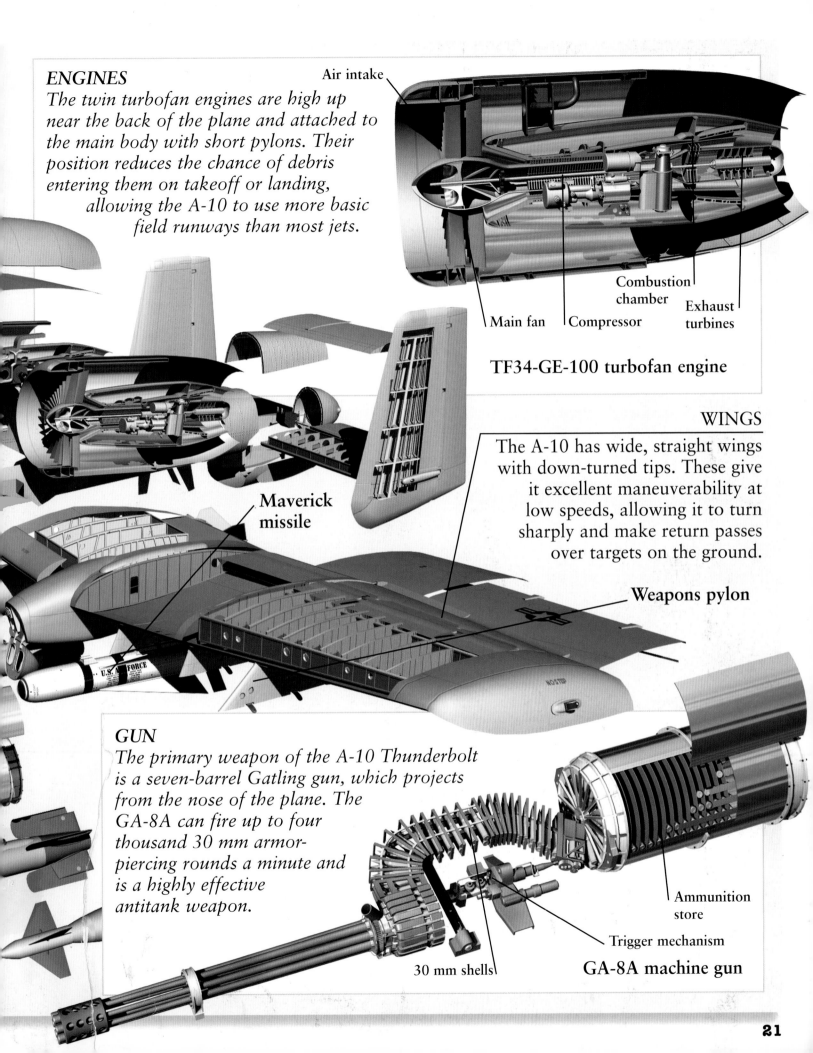

ENGINES

The twin turbofan engines are high up near the back of the plane and attached to the main body with short pylons. Their position reduces the chance of debris entering them on takeoff or landing, allowing the A-10 to use more basic field runways than most jets.

Air intake

Combustion chamber

Exhaust turbines

Main fan   Compressor

TF34-GE-100 turbofan engine

Maverick missile

WINGS

The A-10 has wide, straight wings with down-turned tips. These give it excellent maneuverability at low speeds, allowing it to turn sharply and make return passes over targets on the ground.

Weapons pylon

GUN

The primary weapon of the A-10 Thunderbolt is a seven-barrel Gatling gun, which projects from the nose of the plane. The GA-8A can fire up to four thousand 30 mm armor-piercing rounds a minute and is a highly effective antitank weapon.

Ammunition store

Trigger mechanism

30 mm shells

GA-8A machine gun

EA-6B PROWLER

The EA-6B Prowler is a specialized plane, designed for locating targets by the electromagnetic radiation they give off. All devices that contain electronic equipment give off this radiation. The Prowler can pass this information to other planes or attack the targets itself.

COCKPIT

The cockpit carries four crew members—a pilot and three Electronic Countermeasures Officers (ECMOs). The ECMOs analyze any signals that the Prowler picks up and then convey information to other planes.

CANOPY

The glass within the two-part canopy has a shading of gold to protect the crew from the radio emissions that the Prowler's high-tech equipment gives off.

EA-6B PROWLER

Wingspan: 52.2 feet (15.9 meters)
Length: 58.1 feet (17.7 meters)
Height: 16.1 feet (4.9 meters)
Top speed: 653 mph (1,050 km/h)
Max weapons load: 15,013 pounds (6,810 kilograms)

Ejector seat

Main fuel tank

Mid-air refueling probe

Nose cone

Engine

Fuel drop tank

NOSE RADAR

This is the main device for detecting electromagnetic radiation from enemy targets such as RADAR stations and surface-to-air missile installations.

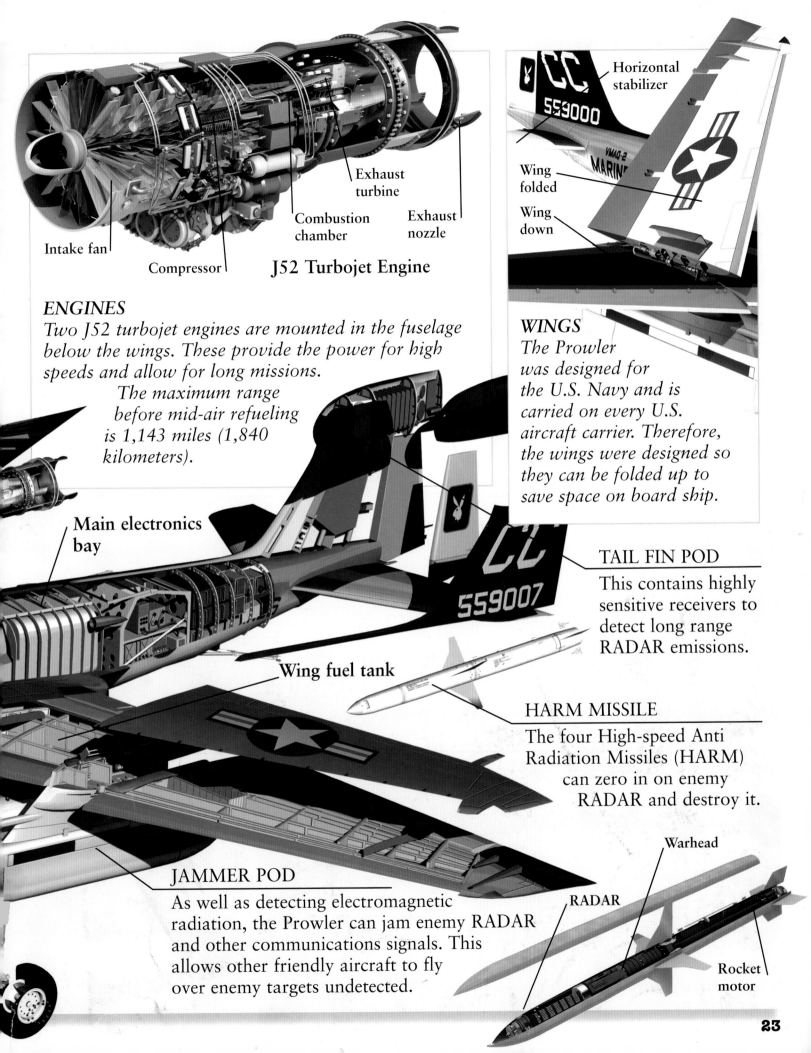

J52 Turbojet Engine

Intake fan

Compressor

Combustion chamber

Exhaust turbine

Exhaust nozzle

Horizontal stabilizer

Wing folded

Wing down

ENGINES

Two J52 turbojet engines are mounted in the fuselage below the wings. These provide the power for high speeds and allow for long missions.

The maximum range before mid-air refueling is 1,143 miles (1,840 kilometers).

WINGS

The Prowler was designed for the U.S. Navy and is carried on every U.S. aircraft carrier. Therefore, the wings were designed so they can be folded up to save space on board ship.

Main electronics bay

Wing fuel tank

TAIL FIN POD

This contains highly sensitive receivers to detect long range RADAR emissions.

HARM MISSILE

The four High-speed Anti Radiation Missiles (HARM) can zero in on enemy RADAR and destroy it.

Warhead

RADAR

JAMMER POD

As well as detecting electromagnetic radiation, the Prowler can jam enemy RADAR and other communications signals. This allows other friendly aircraft to fly over enemy targets undetected.

Rocket motor

MI-24 HIND MILITARY HELICOPTER

Introduced in 1972, the MI-24 Hind Military Helicopter is an assault gunship developed and built in the Soviet Union. It is still used by Russian forces today and by the air forces of more than thirty other nations. The MI-24 has seen active service in numerous conflicts. It is a highly effective gunship that can also act as a troop transporter.

MI-24 HIND MILITARY HELICOPTER

Rotor diameter: 56.8 feet (17.3 meters)
Length: 57.4 feet (17.5 meters)
Height: 21.3 feet (6.5 meters)
Top speed: 208 mph (335 km/h)
Max weapons load: 3,263 pounds (1,480 kilograms)

Exhaust port

ROTOR BLADES

The MI-24 uses a five-blade main rotor driven by two top-mounted engines featuring twin air intakes.

Yak-B 12.7 mm machine gun

COCKPIT

The cockpit seats two or three crew, with the gunner in front of the pilot. It is armored to withstand direct hits from 20 mm rounds.

Engines

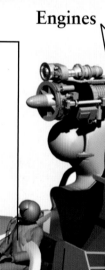

Swivel mount

12.7 MM GUN TURRET

The mobile turret beneath the helicopter's nose carries a four-barrel Gatling gun with 1,470 rounds. The gun is controlled remotely from the cockpit.

Retractable undercarriage

Transport compartment

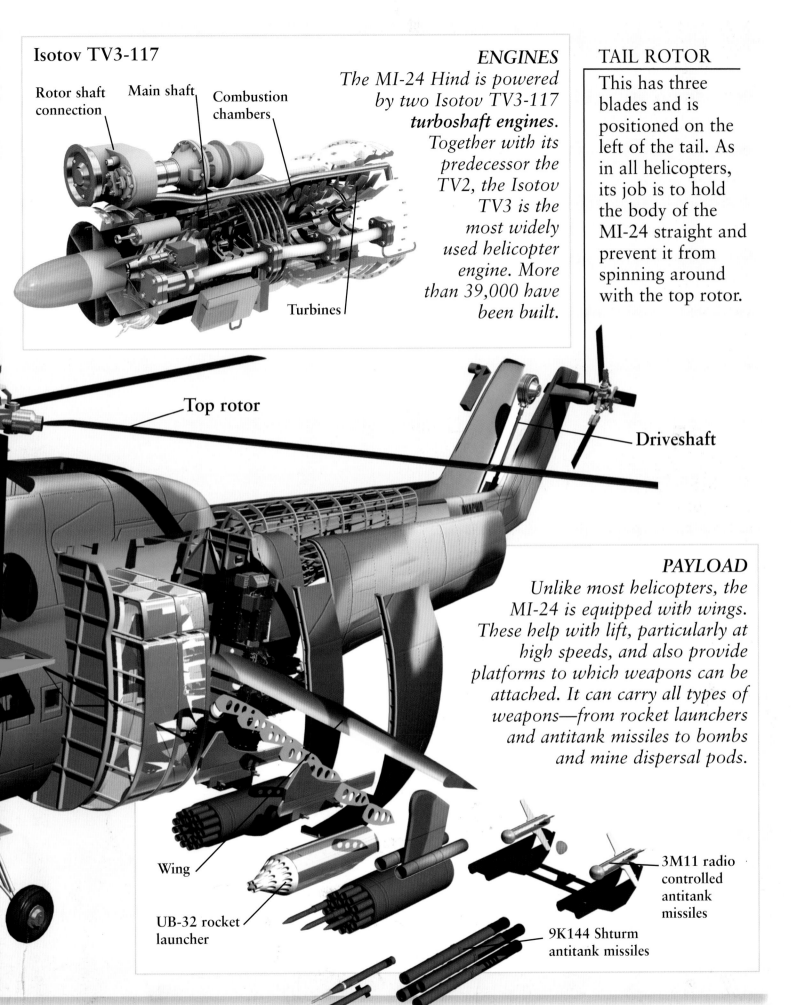

Isotov TV3-117

Rotor shaft connection

Main shaft

Combustion chambers

Turbines

ENGINES

*The MI-24 Hind is powered by two Isotov TV3-117 **turboshaft engines**. Together with its predecessor the TV2, the Isotov TV3 is the most widely used helicopter engine. More than 39,000 have been built.*

TAIL ROTOR

This has three blades and is positioned on the left of the tail. As in all helicopters, its job is to hold the body of the MI-24 straight and prevent it from spinning around with the top rotor.

Top rotor

Driveshaft

PAYLOAD

Unlike most helicopters, the MI-24 is equipped with wings. These help with lift, particularly at high speeds, and also provide platforms to which weapons can be attached. It can carry all types of weapons—from rocket launchers and antitank missiles to bombs and mine dispersal pods.

Wing

UB-32 rocket launcher

3M11 radio controlled antitank missiles

9K144 Shturm antitank missiles

AC-130 SPOOKY GUNSHIP

AC-130 SPECTRE/SPOOKY

Wingspan: 132.5 feet (40.4 meters)
Length: 97.8 feet (29.8 meters)
Height: 38.4 feet (11.7 meters)
Top speed: 298 mph (480 km/h)
Max weapons load: 22,421 pounds (10,170 kilograms)

The AC-130 is a heavily armed ground attack gunship based on the C-130 Hercules transport plane. Used exclusively by the U.S. Air Force, it supports ground troops by firing on hostile forces, and can escort convoys of trucks and other vehicles through dangerous territory.

Ammunition store

Flight deck

Navigation RADAR and moving target indicator

25 MM ROTARY CANNON

The five-barrel Gatling gun can fire up to 1,800 rounds per minute. All of the Spooky's weapons project from the left side of the plane.

Ammunition feed

Night vision RADAR

FIRE CONTROL

The Spooky uses complex targeting technology, including video, infrared, and RADAR sensors. The weapons' firing is controlled from this unit in the plane's center.

Gun barrel

GAU-12/U Equalizer Gatling gun

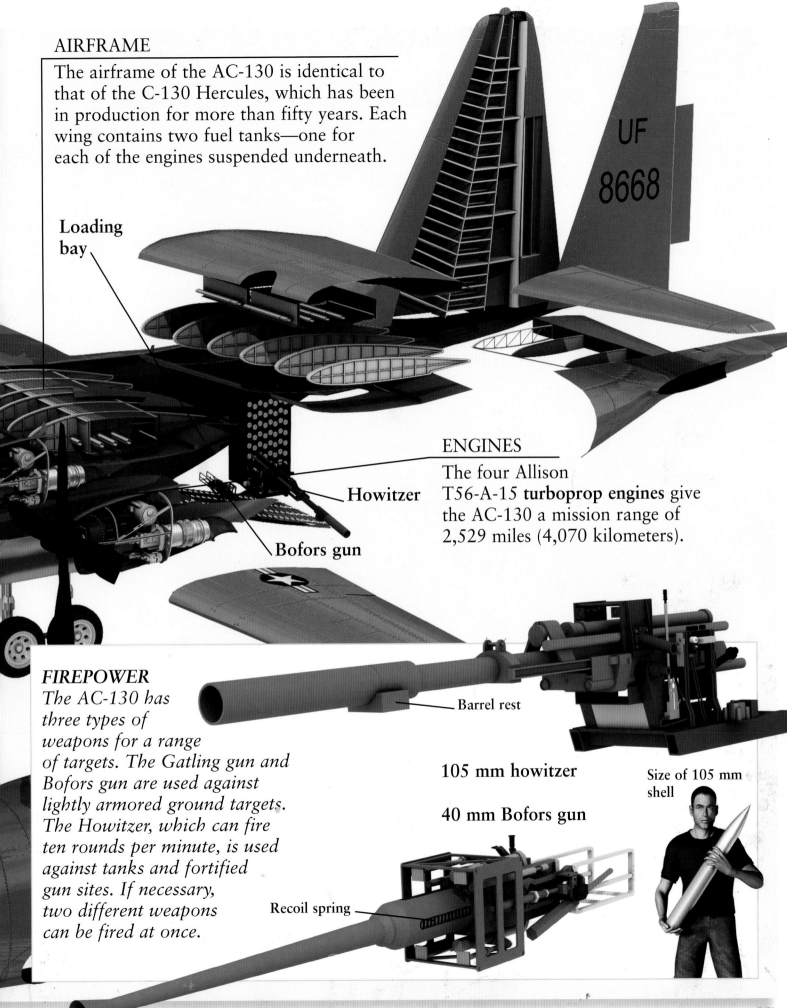

AIRFRAME

The airframe of the AC-130 is identical to that of the C-130 Hercules, which has been in production for more than fifty years. Each wing contains two fuel tanks—one for each of the engines suspended underneath.

Loading bay

UF 8668

ENGINES

The four Allison T56-A-15 **turboprop engines** give the AC-130 a mission range of 2,529 miles (4,070 kilometers).

Howitzer

Bofors gun

Barrel rest

FIREPOWER

The AC-130 has three types of weapons for a range of targets. The Gatling gun and Bofors gun are used against lightly armored ground targets. The Howitzer, which can fire ten rounds per minute, is used against tanks and fortified gun sites. If necessary, two different weapons can be fired at once.

105 mm howitzer

40 mm Bofors gun

Size of 105 mm shell

Recoil spring

27

V-22 OSPREY

The V-22 Osprey began service with the U.S. Marine Corps and Air Force in 2005. It combines the long range and superior speed of a turboprop aircraft with the vertical take-off capability of a helicopter.

Rotor forward flight

ROTORS

At takeoff, the massive rotors are tilted upward. Once airborne, it takes only twelve seconds to rotate the rotors forwards for horizontal flight.

COCKPIT

The large glass canopy in the cockpit offers excellent visibility. Four multi-function display screens with a central display unit show images such as maps and infrared views of the land ahead.

Multi-Function Display Screen

Central Display Unit

V-22 using load hooks in flight

LOAD BAY

Used for carrying troops or supplies, the rear door can open in flight to allow troops to parachute out. The V-22 is equipped with hooks for carrying loads underneath.

Canopy

Wings folded

Props folded

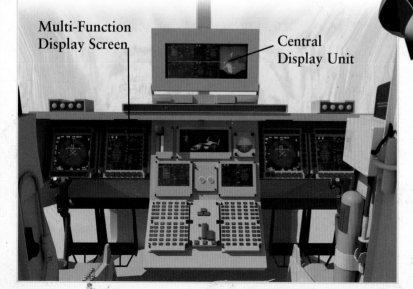

V-22 storage position

V-22 OSPREY

Rotor diameter: 38.1 feet (11.6 meters)
Length: 57.4 feet (17.5 meters)
Height: 22 feet (6.7 meters)
Top speed: 351 mph (565 km/h)
Max weapons load: not applicable

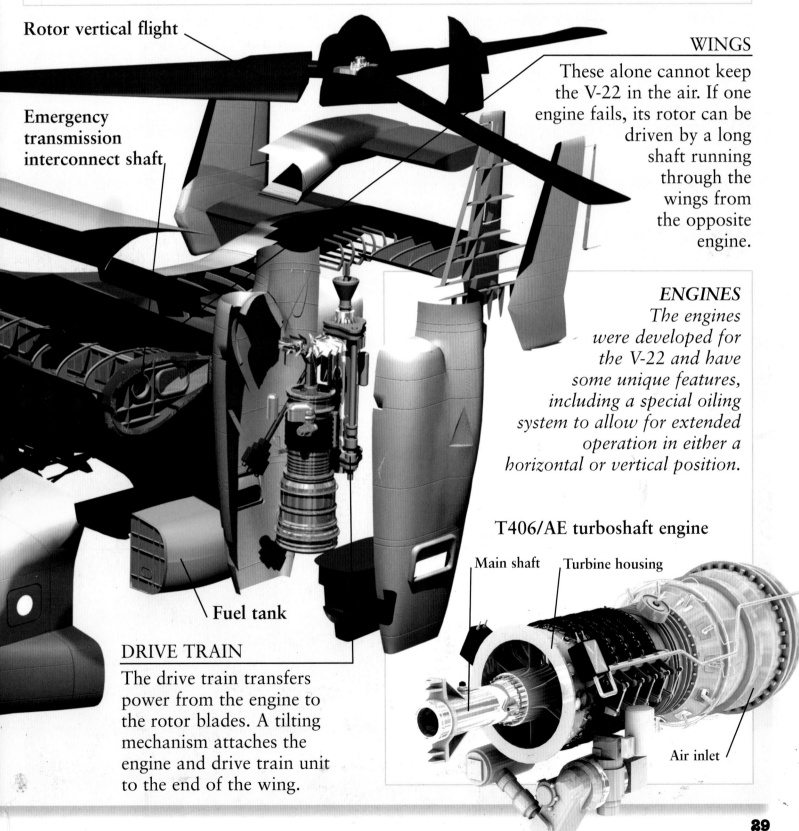

Rotor vertical flight

Emergency transmission interconnect shaft

Fuel tank

WINGS

These alone cannot keep the V-22 in the air. If one engine fails, its rotor can be driven by a long shaft running through the wings from the opposite engine.

ENGINES

The engines were developed for the V-22 and have some unique features, including a special oiling system to allow for extended operation in either a horizontal or vertical position.

T406/AE turboshaft engine

Main shaft   Turbine housing

Air inlet

DRIVE TRAIN

The drive train transfers power from the engine to the rotor blades. A tilting mechanism attaches the engine and drive train unit to the end of the wing.

FUTURE MACHINES

Even as the latest military aircraft enter service, new ones are being developed to replace them. The threat of enemy success means military aircraft design and technology is constantly progressing and aiming to achieve the best performance.

EA-18G GROWLER
This plane will soon enter service with the U.S. Navy. It will escort and "hide" fighter planes by jamming enemy RADAR systems.

PREDATOR
Designed for reconnaissance at medium altitude, this small plane is unmanned.

Modern military aircraft include some of the fastest, most advanced, and most expensive vehicles in the world. Each one is designed and tested over several years before it enters service. These planes show the variety of what we might see in the future.

GLOBAL HAWK
Like the Predator, the Global Hawk is remotely controlled and used for surveillance. However, it is much bigger, and flies at higher altitudes to survey larger areas.

X-45 UCAV
Another unmanned and remotely controlled plane, the X-45, is being developed to undertake bombing missions.

GLOSSARY

afterburner
A jet engine component used to provide a sudden boost in thrust.

airframe
The basic structure of an aircraft.

biplane
A plane with two sets of main wings, one directly above the other.

ejection seat
A seat designed to eject the pilot from the cockpit in an emergency.

electromagnetic radiation
Radiation or waves emitted by objects, including radio, RADAR, microwaves, infrared light, visible light and X-rays.

electro-optical targeting
Targeting using electromagnetic radiation signals.

fuselage
The central body of an aircraft, to which the wings and tail are attached.

head-up display
An electronic display of data superimposed on the inside of the cockpit canopy or the inside of the pilot's visor.

infrared
Electromagnetic radiation just beyond the red end of the light spectrum.

non-orthogonal
Not containing right angles.

RADAR
Ra(dio) d(etection) a(nd) r(anging). A method of detecting objects using very high frequency radio waves.

radome
A dome protecting radar equipment, made from material transparent to radio waves.

reconnaissance.
Exploration to gain information.

stealth technology
Aspects of an aircraft's design that help it avoid detection by radar or other means.

supersonic
Faster than the speed of sound— 761 mph (1,235 km/h).

tilt rotor
An engine and rotor blade assembly that can be tilted from vertical to horizontal.

turbofan engine
A jet engine with a large front fan (intake turbine) that forces air into the engine and also blows air around the engine for extra thrust.

turboprop engine
A turboshaft engine with a gear system to turn a propeller.

turboshaft engine
A jet engine whose central shaft drives another shaft instead of a propellor or fan.

undercarriage
The wheels and landing gear of an aircraft.

INDEX